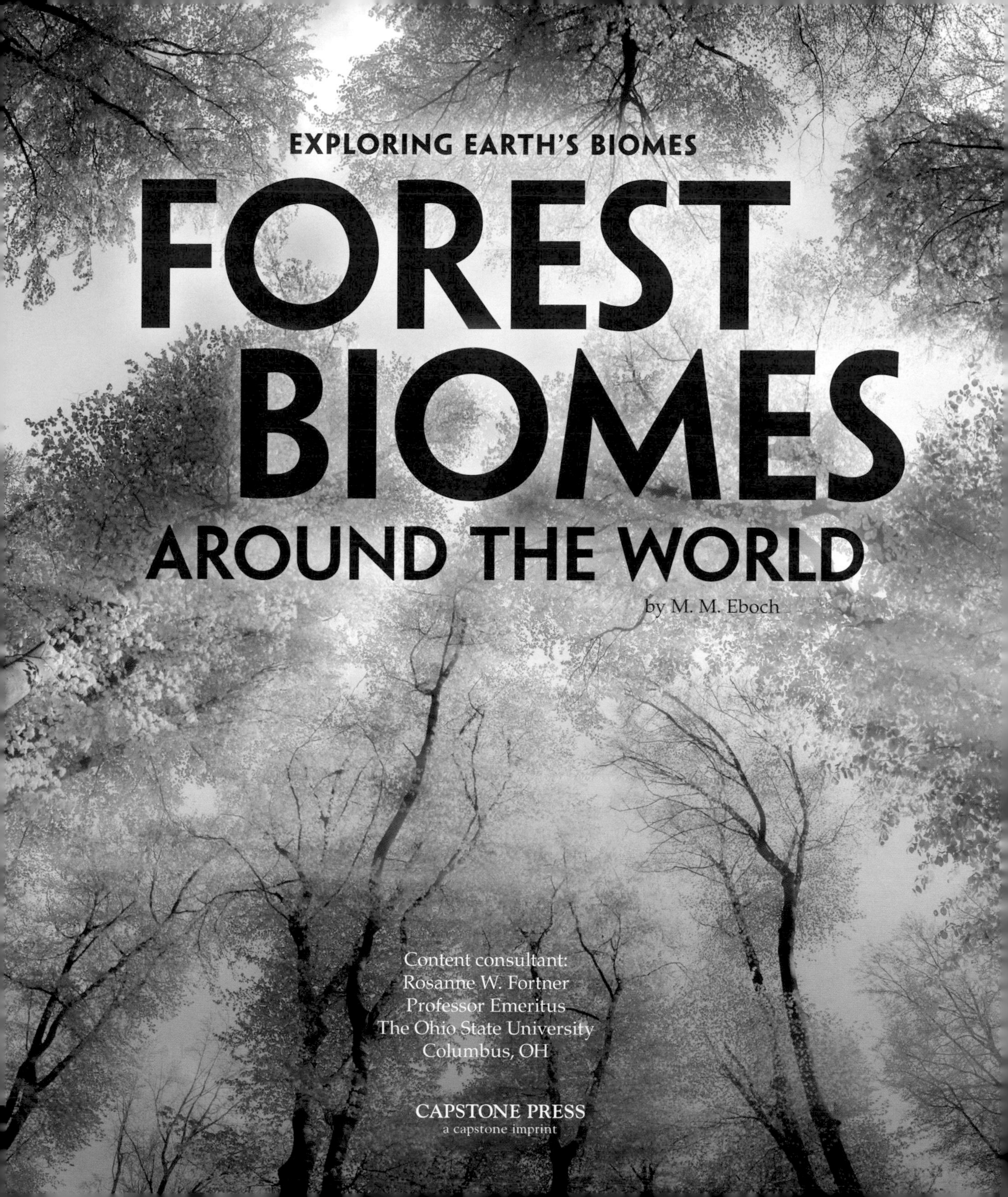

EXPLORING EARTH'S BIOMES

FOREST BIOMES

AROUND THE WORLD

by M. M. Eboch

Content consultant:
Rosanne W. Fortner
Professor Emeritus
The Ohio State University
Columbus, OH

CAPSTONE PRESS
a capstone imprint

Fact Finders Books are published by Capstone Press
1710 Roe Crest Drive, North Mankato, Minnesota 56003
www.capstonepub.com

Library of Congress Cataloging-in-Publication Data
Names: Eboch, M. M., author.
Title: Forest Biomes Around the World / by M. M. Eboch.
Description: North Mankato, Minnesota: Capstone Press, [2020] | Series:
    Fact finders. Exploring Earth's Biomes | Includes index. | Audience: Age
    8–9. | Audience: Grade 4 to 6.
Identifiers: LCCN 2019002053| ISBN 9781543572049 (hardcover) |
    ISBN 9781543575323 (paperback) | ISBN 9781543572162 (ebook pdf)
Subjects: LCSH: Forest ecology—Juvenile literature.
Classification: LCC QH541.5.D4 E264 2020 | DDC 577.3—dc23
LC record available at https://lccn.loc.gov/2019002053

Editorial Credits
Gina Kammer, editor; Julie Peters, designer; Morgan Walters, media researcher;
Kathy McColley, production specialist

Photo Credits
Alamy: Steve Taylor ARPS, bottom 10; Newscom: Ingo Arndt/ Minden Pictures, bottom
12, Staff/The News & Observer, bottom 28, Yingling/MCT, 15; Reuters Pictures: REUTERS
GRAPHICS, 6; Science Source: Gary Hincks, bottom 5; Shutterstock: Andrei Ksenzhuk,
21, Bildagentur Zoonar GmbH, bottom 17, Brandy McKnight, bottom 8, Danita Delmont,
bottom 20, Dariusz Leszczynski, top 23, dugdax, background 8-9, background 10-11,
FedBul, top 25, Gabriel Ostapchuk, background 18-19, background 20-21, background
22-23, isak55, background 12, background 14-15, background 16-17, Jeff Feverston, top 13,
KayaMe, (rainforest) Cover, Lillian Tveit, top right 14, Marten_House, bottom 22, miroslav
chytil, bottom 16, msh11133, background 24-25, background 26-27, pisaphotography, top
19, Radachynskyi Serhii, 24, rodimov, bottom 18, sabri deniz kizil, (floral) Cover, Siarhei
Dzmitryienka, background 4-5, backgorund 6-7, Smileus, background 1, 2-3, 30-31, 32,
(forest) Cover, XiXinXing, (man) Cover, yelantsevv, bottom 26-27

Printed and bound in the USA.
PA70

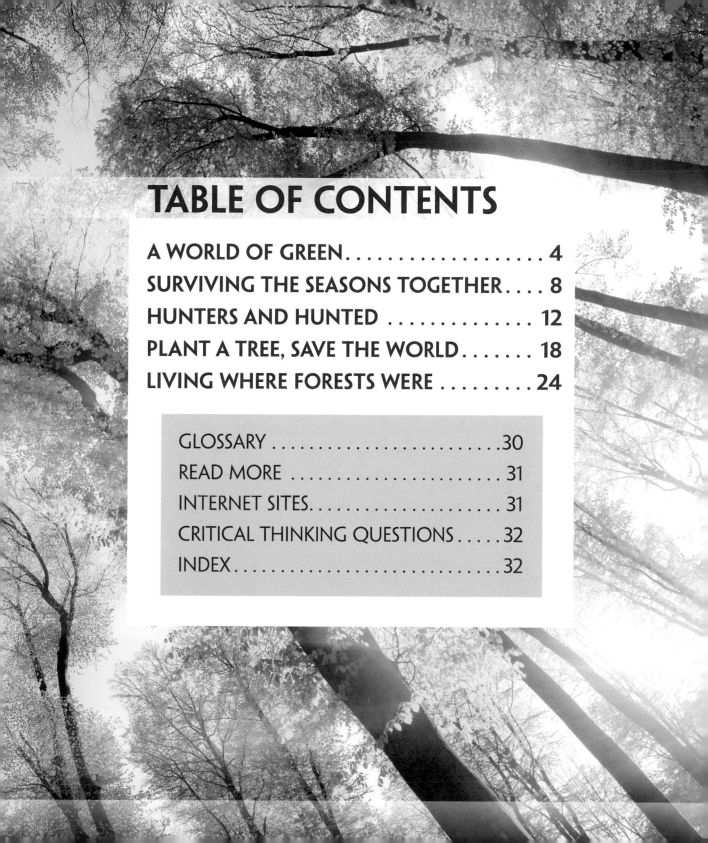

TABLE OF CONTENTS

CHAPTER 1

A WORLD OF GREEN

Imagine walking through a forest during fall. Tall trees grow all around you. Their leaves have turned red, orange, and yellow. Dry leaves crunch under your feet. You're in a **temperate** forest.

Forests are a type of biome. So are deserts, grasslands, tundra, and aquatic. Each type of biome shares a **climate**. Each has animals and plants that can live there. And each biome is important to people and our planet.

Temperate forests have a lot to offer people. Forest soil is good for growing food. Trees provide wood for building and making many products.

TEMPERATE FORESTS

Temperate forests are one of the three main types of forests in the forest biome. Tropical forests stay hot and green all year. Boreal forests have long winters and short, cool summers. However, a temperate forest is sometimes hot and sometimes cold. Temperate forests aren't found near the cold poles or the hot equator. They flourish in the temperate zone between those two regions.

FACT BOX
Forests cover about 30 percent of Earth's land.

Forest Biomes Around the World

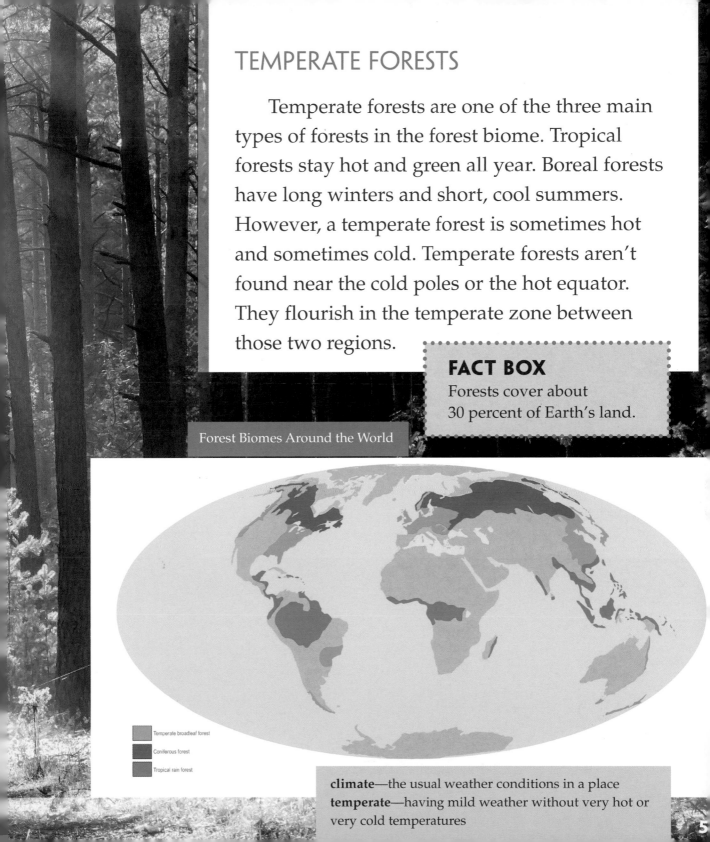

- Temperate broadleaf forest
- Coniferous forest
- Tropical rain forest

climate—the usual weather conditions in a place
temperate—having mild weather without very hot or very cold temperatures

5

THE FOUR SEASONS

A temperate forest has four separate seasons. In spring, the temperature rises. In some temperate forests, the **precipitation** levels also increase. Young leaves and flowers appear. Plants grow most during the heat of summer. Leaves capture sunlight to make food. In fall, temperatures drop. Precipitation can also decrease in some areas. Leaves change color. They dry up and fall from the trees. Winter may bring snow and freezing temperatures.

The forest biome used to cover half of Earth's land. Around the world, people cut down forests to use the trees and farm the rich soil. Forested land shrank by 20 percent. Today, a quarter of what's left is temperate forest.

precipitation—moisture that lands on the ground, including rain, snow, mist, or fog

The Eastern Deciduous Forest used to cover much of the eastern United States. It stretches from southern Canada to Florida. Parts go as far west as Texas and Minnesota. However, it's no longer one big forest. When European settlers arrived, people cleared the forest to make room for towns and farms. They cut down trees for firewood and building material. They built dams along rivers. Mills used the water's power to grind grain or cut logs. Only about 0.1 percent of this forest was never changed by humans.

DECLINING FOREST COVER

DEFORESTATION INDEX
Data evaluated for forest cover between 2005-2010

Risk level:

■ Extreme   ■ High   ■ Medium   ■ Low   ■ No data

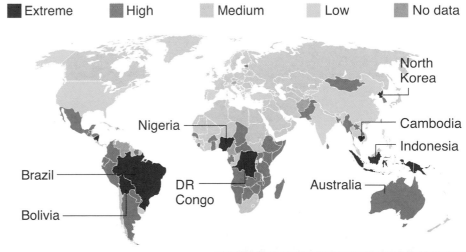

North Korea

Nigeria

Cambodia

Indonesia

Brazil

DR Congo

Australia

Bolivia

Tropical forests are one of the most common areas where trees are cut down.

CHAPTER 2

SURVIVING THE SEASONS TOGETHER

Like people, plants and animals **adapt** to the biomes where they live. In temperate forests, many plants must withstand cold winters. **Deciduous** trees such as oak, elm, ash, and beech drop their leaves during fall. This helps the tree conserve its energy during winter. The forest floor is covered with dead leaves. Snails, earthworms, flies, and beetles help break down dead leaves. The leaves then become food for the forest.

an earthworm

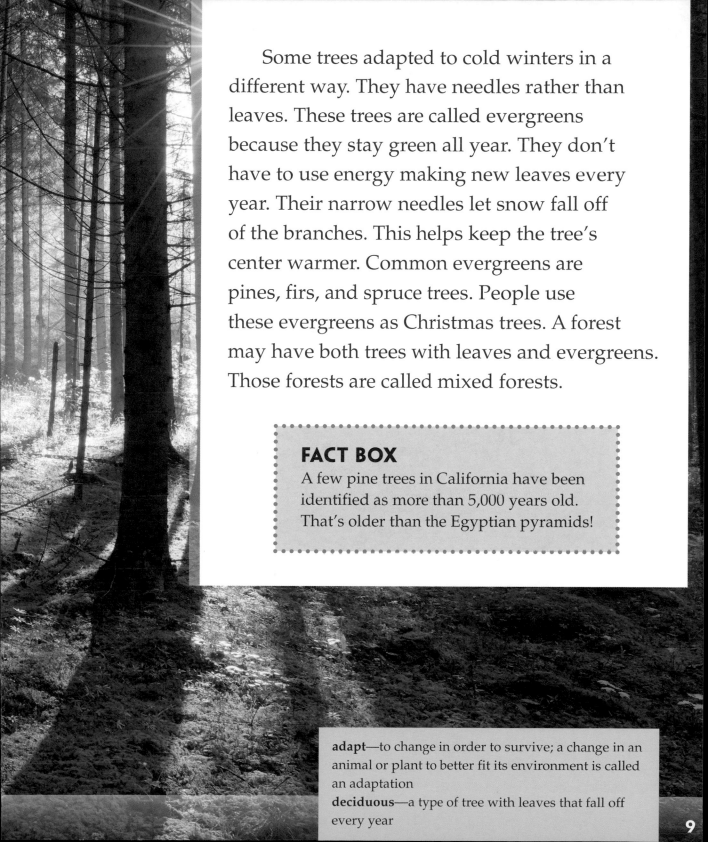

Some trees adapted to cold winters in a different way. They have needles rather than leaves. These trees are called evergreens because they stay green all year. They don't have to use energy making new leaves every year. Their narrow needles let snow fall off of the branches. This helps keep the tree's center warmer. Common evergreens are pines, firs, and spruce trees. People use these evergreens as Christmas trees. A forest may have both trees with leaves and evergreens. Those forests are called mixed forests.

FACT BOX

A few pine trees in California have been identified as more than 5,000 years old. That's older than the Egyptian pyramids!

adapt—to change in order to survive; a change in an animal or plant to better fit its environment is called an adaptation

deciduous—a type of tree with leaves that fall off every year

Oak trees may live for centuries because they grow very slowly. The slow growth helps them survive low light and dry seasons. In England, legend says that the outlaw hero Robin Hood lived in Sherwood Forest. Today Sherwood Forest holds more than 900 big oak trees. One of Sherwood Forest's oaks may be 1,000 years old. The stories say this massive oak was a meeting place for Robin Hood and his friends.

a large oak tree in Sherwood Forest in England

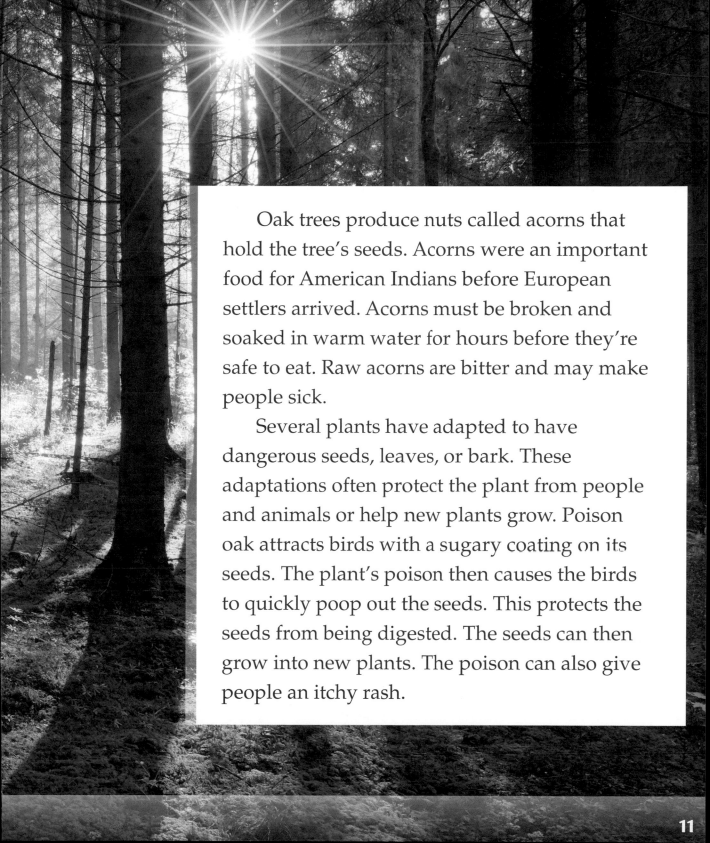

Oak trees produce nuts called acorns that hold the tree's seeds. Acorns were an important food for American Indians before European settlers arrived. Acorns must be broken and soaked in warm water for hours before they're safe to eat. Raw acorns are bitter and may make people sick.

Several plants have adapted to have dangerous seeds, leaves, or bark. These adaptations often protect the plant from people and animals or help new plants grow. Poison oak attracts birds with a sugary coating on its seeds. The plant's poison then causes the birds to quickly poop out the seeds. This protects the seeds from being digested. The seeds can then grow into new plants. The poison can also give people an itchy rash.

CHAPTER 3

HUNTERS
AND HUNTED

Temperate forests are home to deer, foxes, raccoons, skunks, rabbits, and birds. All these animals must deal with warm summers and cold winters. Some, including butterflies and some birds, **migrate** to avoid winter. Some animals hide food for later. Squirrels and chipmunks gather nuts in the fall. They store them to eat in winter, when food is hard to find. Other animals **hibernate**. Black bears, toads, frogs, snakes, and turtles rest in winter so they don't need to find food.

A mother black bear and her cub hibernate in the winter.

a doe in winter

While deer don't hibernate, they are less active during winter. They may not move for several days, living off their stored fat. Deer prepare for winter by growing thick, heavy coats. Their winter coat is darker, so it absorbs more sunlight for warmth. A deer's skin produces oil, which helps its fur stay dry in the snow.

hibernate—to go into a resting state over the winter, as if in a deep sleep
migrate—to travel from one area to another on a regular basis

Gray wolves have adapted to hunt deer in winter. The wolves have strong jaws for killing and eating large animals. Wolves also have thick coats to protect them from the cold. They have good hearing and night vision. Their sense of smell is 100 times better than a human's.

gray wolves

People often fear wolves, even though they rarely harm humans. Hunters don't want wolves to kill game animals such as deer. Farmers and ranchers worry that wolves will kill farm animals. Wolves once roamed throughout North American forests. Then people began hunting wolves. In many areas, wolves were wiped out. Only a small population was left in the northern Midwest by the mid-1900s. In 1973, laws began protecting wolves. Their numbers grew, but far fewer wolves live now than in the past.

Today many of the laws protecting wolves have ended. More wolves are being killed again.

AMERICAN GRAY WOLF DISTRIBUTION

Hunting virtually eliminated gray wolves from the western U.S. by the 1930s. The Endangered Species Act offered Canis lupus federal protection in 1973, and wolves were reintroduced to Yellowstone National Park more than 20 years later.

Wolf distribution

■ Current range ■ Historic range

Western Great Lakes population

Wash.

Mont.

Ore.

Minn.

Idaho   Wyo.   Wis.   Mich.

Northern Rocky Mountain population

Ariz.   N.M.

Mexican wolf population

Gray wolf
Canis lupus

Gray wolf populations began to climb once again after they were listed as endangered in the 1970s.

KEEPING THE BALANCE

People still fear wolves. But wolves have a valuable role in nature. They're a **keystone species**, meaning they're very important to their environment. Wolves help control the numbers of other animals. Without wolves as hunters, animal populations can grow out of control.

gray wolves in winter

Wolves, bears, and mountain lions used to control the deer population. Today many of these large predators are gone. The deer population has greatly increased. More deer live in North America today than ever before. Too many deer can harm a forest. Deer don't hibernate in winter. They eat anything they can find, including new buds on trees. They eat plants that other animals, such as songbirds, need. Deer can also cause car accidents and spread diseases to people.

People can help keep animal species in balance. One way is to let large animals such as wolves hunt freely. Hunting laws can also help manage animal numbers.

American red wolves

FACT BOX
Wolves communicate by howling. A pack may howl together to say, "This is our territory."

keystone species—a species so important that losing it would hurt other species

CHAPTER 4

PLANT A TREE, SAVE THE WORLD

Forests benefit people in many ways. Forests provide **timber**. Timber can be made into writing paper, toilet paper, paper towels, and much more. Forests provide food too. Some people hunt forest animals, such as turkey or deer. Temperate forests also have many nuts and berries. Forest mushrooms can be poisonous, but some types are good for food.

timber—wood from trees used for building and making things

Many people gather in Central Park in New York City.

Trees and plants provide another very important thing—oxygen. Oxygen is the most important part of the air we breathe. Forests near highways reduce the noise and pollution from cars. Cleaner air means healthier people. Forests in city parks make the city prettier and attract visitors. The trees provide shade that helps keep the city cooler in summer.

Temperate forests also provide homes for many animals. New species of plants and animals are found each year.

Scientists announced a new species of hemlock tree in 2017. It's found only in temperate forests in Korea. Hemlocks are homes for some insects and birds. In the eastern United States, an insect from Japan is killing the hemlocks. However, the insects don't kill the Korean trees. Scientists are studying the Korean hemlocks to learn how to save American trees. If that fails, the Korean hemlocks may be planted in place of the dying trees.

a hemlock grove in New Hampshire

Other new species might be good for food or have other benefits to humans. Many plants and animals are used in medicines, so a new species could save lives. Cutting down a forest could wipe out a new species before anyone finds it.

Young puffball mushrooms can be safe to eat, but many types are deadly. Only mushroom experts should gather wild mushrooms.

THE LOST FOREST

Some forests have been completely cut down. This process is known as clear-cutting. The loss of forests is called **deforestation**. Cleared land may be needed for growing crops or grazing farm animals. People may want to use the timber. However, deforestation causes problems. The trees that made oxygen are gone. Animals lose their homes. Rain washes away the exposed soil. The dirt can flow into rivers and harm fish. Yet, we need trees for building and making paper products. What can we do?

an area of pine trees is cut down in Scotland

deforestation—the cutting down of forests

Forests can be thinned without clear-cutting. Trees can be removed when they are old and no longer healthy. That leaves room for younger trees to grow. The forest continues, and we keep benefiting from it.

cut logs are ready to be picked up and taken out of the forest

CHAPTER 5

LIVING WHERE FORESTS WERE

Was your town or city once a forest?

Early people lived by hunting and gathering wild foods. Forests were ideal homes for hunter-gatherers. It isn't too hot or too cold. The land is good for growing food. Rainfall and streams provide water.

However, actually living in a forest is challenging. The thick stands of trees make it hard to build houses, plant crops, or travel. Often people cut down the trees to clear land. Then they build houses, plant crops, and build towns. Over time, towns grow into cities. Yet some people manage to live in forests as they are. They might live in small cabins far from towns. They may hunt and gather food from the forest or plant their own crops like the early people.

a cabin home in the woods

Only stumps are left after trees are cleared in an area of forest.

America still has many forests, but they've changed. When trees are cut down for logging, different types of trees may replace them. The changed forest might not be as healthy. It might not have the same animals and plants. When forests appear in smaller patches, wild animals have less room to move freely.

CHANGING CLIMATE

Pollution also hurts forests. High levels of pollution stunt or stop plant growth. **Climate change** affects temperature, rainfall, and weather. An area may become too hot or too dry for the plants and animals that live there. Some species may move to new areas. Other plants and animals may die out as the climate warms.

A warmer climate can also result in more storms and fires that damage forests. Every year wildfires destroy millions of acres of U.S. forests. Climate change may bring more and deadlier wildfires.

climate change—a significant change in Earth's climate over a period of time

Climate change also affects insects. Insects are a key part of the forest biome. They help plants make seeds. But not all insects are good for forests. Some insects weaken or kill trees. Beetles and moths have killed huge patches of forest. Climate change causes higher temperatures. This change lets some insects grow faster and move into new areas.

FACT BOX

Wildfires are part of nature. Some trees and plants need fire for their best growth. Today people often try to control fires, which changes which plants grow in forests.

Temperature changes can also encourage the growth of **invasive species**. These plants or animals are new to an area. The **native species** may not be able to compete. Invasive species can take over, while native species die out. The Japanese insect killing hemlock trees, the hemlock woolly adelgid, is an invasive species.

Controlling a tree killer

The hemlock woolly adelgid, an exotic pest, is killing two species of hemlock, the eastern and Carolina, from Georgia to Maine.

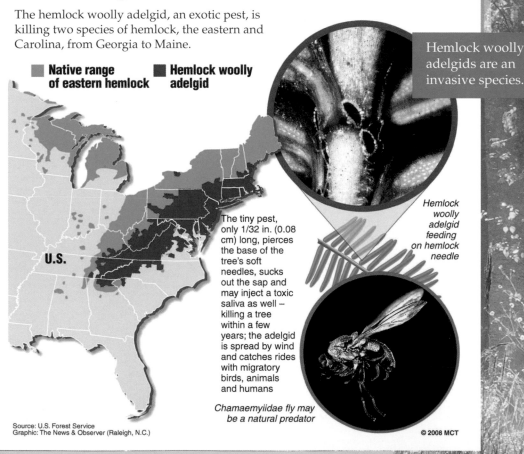

■ **Native range of eastern hemlock**   ■ **Hemlock woolly adelgid**

U.S.

The tiny pest, only 1/32 in. (0.08 cm) long, pierces the base of the tree's soft needles, sucks out the sap and may inject a toxic saliva as well — killing a tree within a few years; the adelgid is spread by wind and catches rides with migratory birds, animals and humans

Hemlock woolly adelgids are an invasive species.

Hemlock woolly adelgid feeding on hemlock needle

Chamaemyiidae fly may be a natural predator

Source: U.S. Forest Service
Graphic: The News & Observer (Raleigh, N.C.)

© 2008 MCT

invasive species—a species new to an area, which may spread easily and cause harm
native species—a species that lives and grows naturally in a particular region without the help of humans

SAVING THE FORESTS

There is hope for forests. They can grow back if given the chance, but this process takes many years. People can help by planting new trees. The European country of Iceland lost almost all its forests. Now people there are planting about 3 million new trees every year. The United Kingdom's government is planning to plant a new forest across the country. It should one day be a ribbon of 50 million new trees. Robin Hood would be glad!

U.S. groups are also trying to plant more trees. They hope to replace deforestation with **reforestation**. That means more trees for healthy forests. Healthy forests help people and the planet stay healthy. That's good for every species.

FACT BOX

What can you do? Fighting climate change is a good way to protect every biome. You can help. Think "reduce, reuse, recycle." Reduce what you use by buying less. Get used clothes and toys from a thrift store. Use things for as long as you can. When you can no longer use something, recycle it.

Take extra care with paper products. Most paper comes from trees. You can buy recycled paper. Use both sides of a piece of paper, and then recycle it. Avoid paper plates, cups, and towels that get thrown away. Instead, buy products you can use again.

reforestation—the process of planting trees where original trees were cut down

GLOSSARY

adapt (uh-DAPT)—to change in order to survive; a change in an animal or plant to better fit its environment is called an adaptation

climate (KLY-muht)—the usual weather conditions in a place

climate change (KLY-muht CHAYNJ)—a significant change in Earth's climate over a period of time

deciduous (dih-SIJ-oo-uhs)—a type of tree with leaves that fall off every year

deforestation (dee-for-uh-STAY-shuhn)—the cutting down of forests

hibernate (HYE-bur-nate)—to go into a resting state over the winter, as if in a deep sleep

invasive species (in-VAY-suhv SPEE-sheez)—a species new to an area, which may spread easily and cause harm

keystone species (KEE-stohn SPEE-sheez)—a species so important that losing it would hurt other species

migrate (MYE-grate)—to travel from one area to another on a regular basis

native species (NAY-tuhv SPEE-sheez)—a species that lives and grows naturally in a particular region without the help of humans

precipitation (pree-sip-i-TAY-shuhn)—moisture that lands on the ground, including rain, snow, mist, or fog

reforestation (ree-for-uh-STAY-shuhn)—the process of planting trees where original trees were cut down

temperate (TEM-pur-it)—having mild weather without very hot or very cold temperatures

timber (TIM-bur)—wood from trees used for building and making things

READ MORE

Boothroyd, Jennifer. *Let's Visit the Deciduous Forest.* Biome Explorers. Minneapolis: Lerner Publications, 2017.

Johansson, Philip. *The Temperate Forest: Discover This Wooded Biome.* Discover the World's Biomes. Berkeley Heights, NJ: Enslow Elementary, 2015.

Silverman, Buffy. *Let's Visit the Evergreen Forest.* Biome Explorers. Minneapolis: Lerner Publications, 2017.

Spilsbury, Louise A., and Richard Spilsbury. *Forest Biomes.* Earth's Natural Biomes. New York: Crabtree Publishing Company, 2017.

INTERNET SITES

Kids Do Ecology: Temperate Forest
http://kids.nceas.ucsb.edu/biomes/temperateforest.html

Kidzworld: Biomes of the World: Forests
https://www.kidzworld.com/article/2115-biomes-of-the-world-forests

National Geographic Kids: Temperate Forest
https://kids.nationalgeographic.com/explore/nature/habitats/temperate-forest/

National Park Service: Eastern Deciduous Forest
https://www.nps.gov/im/ncrn/eastern-deciduous-forest.htm

CRITICAL THINKING QUESTIONS

1. Plants and animals can help humans in many ways. Is that a good reason to protect nature? What are other reasons? Which is most important?
2. Many people are afraid of wolves. They kill a small number of farm animals each year. Should wolves be killed to protect people and farm animals? Or should wolves be protected by law? Why?
3. Climate change is affecting where plants and animals can live. Invasive species are killing off some native species. How important is it to keep things the same? Should we simply let these changes happen? Explain your answer.

INDEX